KINGDOM

THE RISE OF THE CREATIVE CHURCH

eBook and audiobook also availible

Soli Deo Gloria.
To God alone be the glory.

VOLUME I
BARA
The artistic heritage

VOLUME II
PHOS
The light of the culture

VOLUME III
POIEMA
The Portraits

All Bible segments are quoted from the
New King James Version unless stated otherwise.

VOLUME I

BARA

THE ARTISTIC HERITAGE

CHAPTER ONE

UNTHINKABLE

It is ridiculous
for a believer to say they have no creative bone in their body.

Unfathomable.

If they only knew the rich stream of genius that
flows throughout their heritage,
they would deeply reconsider.

Let me show you where your creativity comes from.

"In the beginning God created the heavens and the earth."
Genesis 1:1 - one of the most overlooked scriptures ever written.

But think about it.
The ground you stand on,
the skies you gaze at,
the very earth you live in,
was non-existent until God thought it.

Outside of Him was pitch-blackness,
and it spread endlessly from the left,
to the right,
behind and before.

But residing inside of Him was an idea most controversial.
A Master-plan.
He smiled to Himself,
as He thought to do The Unthinkable.

In the silence, a command was given.
This audible command, which echoed throughout space,
changed everything, forever.

"LET THERE BE LIGHT".

The moment He spoke it,
time began.

0000:000:00:00:01

An hourglass,
of which He could see the end of time
as clear as the beginning.
He said to Himself that it was good.

He spent the next five days continuing to create.
Setting the stage,
preparing for The Unthinkable.

"In the beginning God *created* the
heavens
and the earth."
Read the same sentence again in Hebrew.

The word *'created'* in Hebrew is

BARA.

What is BARA? It means simply 'to create'. But it is interesting because the word is only used in scriptures that refer to God. Why? Because God is the only one who can create something without using existing materials.

Before God said, "LET THERE BE LIGHT", light was unimaginable. It was an impossible concept. Time was an unreasonable theory, until God thought it. All original ideas are firstly a thought of God.

If He never thought it, then it does not exist.

We call Him "God", the origin of creativity.

His complexity is unmatched.
From the minutely small strands of DNA,
to the infinitely magnificent galaxies of the universe,
he has given it all unique design,
and it is all designed beautifully.

His creative abundance is unsurpassed.
He continually creates,
yet refuses to make the same thing twice.

He invents all kinds of planets in all kinds of colours,
including this planet,
which we call Earth.

Earth has a sky, which paints all kinds of paintings,
and below these skies are all kinds of mammals.

Deep down in the sea are all kinds of fish,
which feed on all kinds of foods.
Some sweet,
some savoury.
There are all kinds of flavours
and all kinds of nutrients.

Some big,
some small.
Life in all kinds of sizes.
And every living thing can reproduce.

There are trees hidden in seeds.
There are babies hidden in humans.

Earth is a living and breathing blue ball
which hangs perfectly in the middle of nothing.
But yet, it is self-sufficient.
"Abundance" is not even an accurate term.

Whoever lives here would never
need to leave the planet for a single resource.

And it is all His work.
He collaborated with nobody.

He needed no mentorship.
He needed no peer groups.
He needed no inspiration.

He is inspiration.

God is not the most creative being,
God is the *only* creative being.

OMNIPOTENT
(All energy and power)

OMNISCIENT
(All science and knowledge)

And through it all, His creativity never exhausts itself.
These few days of creation were just a warm up.
Mere decoration.
By-products of the Master-plan.

It was empty, six days ago,
now look.

It was silent, six days ago,
now the oceans roar,
and the thunders clap,
and the trees rustle their leaves,
and the birds sing their songs.

The Sun lights up the Earth
like stage lights do an opening act,
as all creation witnesses God
as He begins to work on His Masterpiece.

The time is now set for Him to do The Unthinkable.

CHAPTER TWO

A BODY OF WORK

THE SOLO EXHIBITION

God is an artist,
and like any other artist,
he signs His name on His works.

His signature style can be found on every created thing.

"For since the creation of the world
His invisible attributes are clearly seen,
being understood by the things that are made,
even His eternal power and Godhead,
so that they are without excuse…" *Romans 1:20*

The lions display His boldness.
The lambs display His humility.
The oceans display His depths.
The skies display His superiority.
The colours of the flower fields display His vibrancy.
The design of the fruits displays His ingenuity.

Look around you,
God is hidden in plain sight.

There was, however, one disadvantage.
These created works could only display
one Godly trait each.
Nothing in the universe
was able to exhibit all of God's character.

Not one art piece could carry His boldness,
His superiority,
His authority,
His vibrancy,
and His creativity
all at one time.

Until the sixth day,
when God decided to create a body of work.

A Masterpiece
that encapsulated all of His character into one grand design.
God normally spoke things into being.
"Let there be" this
or "let there be" that.
But when God thought to do The Unthinkable,
He said "let *Us* make man in Our own image".

He dug deep into the soil with His own hands,
and began to make and mould.
Bone by bone.
Limb by limb.
Eyelash by eyelash.

This man was the sum of three components:

THE BODY
Interaction with the outside world

THE SOUL
Interaction with self

THE SPIRIT
Interaction with God

From the laugh,
to the fingerprint,
it was all intimately designed,
and when He looked at it, He said it was good.
He stared at Adam as if He beheld Himself in the mirror.

Man: The self-portrait of God

For the first time in history,
God had someone He was comfortable collaborating with.
God would provide the materials,
and man would have the innate imagination
and creativity to see his heart desires materialise.

Earth was a playground,
but only for a time.

I suppose our gift and curse is one and the same:
choice.

Before man,
choice belonged to God alone.

At God's command,
the sea only goes past a certain point.
The sun stays exactly where it is.
Not and inch closer, not an inch further away.
But God can command us to love Him,
and we can say "no".

And one day we did just that,
when we thought we had no more use for God,
and our teeth sunk deep into the sweet forbidden fruit.
The juices of its consequence absorbed into our bloodstreams.
Trickling down into our very soul.
Infecting our very genetics.

Sin,
changing us from The Unthinkable,
to the non-presentable.
An art piece gone horrifically wrong.
And what does an artist do to an art piece that is beyond repair?

Earth went from playground to graveyard.

Sin continues to poison our bloodlines till this day.
Human beings are birthed into this world crying.
They spend their entire lives in pain,
then die hopeless.

We divorced God,
and asked for full custody of His creativity and materials,
so we could continue to build our pyramids and skyscrapers,
cities and empires,
all by ourselves.
Attempting to build back the paradise we lost.

But true creativity and ingenuity left us.
Only traces remain.

The gap between the faces of the deep,
and the roof of the universe,
was the distance between God and man.

But God continues to watch from afar
at this blue ball that hangs in the middle of nothing.

Carefully thinking of ways to restore
before the blue
fades to grey.

CHAPTER THREE

MASTER OF THE
ARTS

THE EMPOWERMENT OF
BEZALEL

Traces remain.
Traces remain.
True creativity is lost,
and only traces remain.

God found His gateway back to earth.
A nation.
And He called this nation the Israelites.

They were despised above all people,
but yet they were adopted to be the children of God.

And He loved them like a Father,
but long distance relationships could never do.
He wanted to get closer,
so He decided to behold His own power and extinguish it;
squeezing Himself into a tent
(or a tabernacle)
just so He could be in the same room as His people.

That was the idea,
yet one questioned lingered in the air,
who could build such a tabernacle?

God needed an architect,
but the Israelites had just escaped Egypt,
being victim to four hundred years of slavery.
So anything they created would have been tainted
with Egyptian culture;
a culture that *stood* for everything God is *against*.

God would not settle for that.
It needed to be a tabernacle fit for a King.

Such a place could only be created
if such a place was designed by God Himself.

But then again,
even if God gave a willing heart the blueprints to this design,
the question *still* lingers:

Who would be able to build such a thing,
if only traces remain?

"I have called by name Bezalel the son of Uri, the son of Hur,
of the tribe of Judah.
And I have filled him with the Spirit of God,
in wisdom,
in understanding,
in knowledge,
and in all manner of workmanship,
to design artistic works…" *Exodus 31:2-4a*

Bezalel, God's first commissioned artist.

He had to follow God's instructions down to the very last detail.
The dimensions,
the materials that were to be used,
the artefacts that needed to be crafted.
There was no room for Egyptian influence.

The layout of the tabernacle was split into three:

THE OUTER COURT
Where the public offered sacrifices

THE INNER COURT
Where the priests exclusively worshipped

THE HOLY OF HOLIES
Where the power and presence of God Himself resided

The task was vast,
but he was not left helpless.
He was filled with God's Spirit.

RUACH

is the Hebrew word for it.
'The breath of God'.

The same breath that said "LET THERE BE LIGHT".
The same breath that moulded the known galaxies.
The same breath that made man a living creature.
This all-creative Spirit,
is now in this one artist.

Bezalel, the master of the arts.

In an instant,
he became a goldsmith,
an engraver,
a carpenter,
a dressmaker,
a stonecutter,
a weaver,
an interior designer,
and an embroiderer.

It would have taken many a lifetime to master one of these skills.
Not Bezalel.

And it is interesting,
Exodus 31:2 would be one of the first mentions in scripture
where God says He would fill someone with His Spirit.

It is comforting to know
that one of the first Spirit-filled persons on the planet
was an artist.

He was filled with all wisdom,
understanding,
knowledge,
and the ability to master any craft conceivable.

No more traces.
Creative restoration is here.

And from that day forward,
the people could never again say they lacked skill.
God could make anybody a world-class artist from then on.

He gave the people dreams and visions.
He taught them with symbolism and metaphor.
He expressed to them His thoughts,
and they poetically wrote it down on scrolls.

The Hebrews became visual learners
and it showed in their writing.
Not rhyming with words,
but rhyming with ideas.
Explaining the majesty of God
by the beauty of His creation.

They wrote with poetic flair,
because they believed
that if something of such importance was to be said,
it was to be said beautifully.

So when you open up the scriptures,
know that it is not a mere instruction manual you gaze upon,
it is God's sketchbook.
His poetry to us,
His ideas and concepts,
His beautiful illustrations,
His designs and redesigns of mankind,
His architectural plans of building Eden back on earth.

And the final result was beyond words,
the tabernacle, I mean.
I wonder how it felt
to know that you have built a home for God.

It incorporated every art form imaginable,
but the temple was not made for art's sake alone.

This is known by one of Bezalel's greatest creations
found at the heart of the Holy Of Holies.
One of the most desired artefacts in human history.
The golden crate of two cherubims,
known as the Ark of the Covenant.

This was not just a beautiful work of craftsmanship,
this was a symbol of the King's presence,
a contract between God and man,
a promise that all will be restored.

It reminded the Israelites
that despite living in a godless world,
as long as the ark remains,
His presence would be there too.

CHAPTER FOUR

BURNOUT

THE RELENTLESSNESS
OF DAVID

The Ark of the Covenant is missing.

Years have past,
and the Israelites have forgotten themselves.

They have all fallen back into their old barbaric state,
and when the people's spirituality decays,
so does their creativity.

Compared to surrounding nations,
their technology was embarrassing.
Their enemies encircled them with swords and spears,
while they awkwardly fought back
with bows and slingshots.

Read 1 Samuel 13:19-22.
Only two swords were found in the entire military force.
They were completely unequipped.

There was not a single blacksmith in the land to
mould weapons of iron.
Thank the Philistines for that.
They claimed ownership over that particular trade.
So all things war and agriculture,
would have been dealt with on Philistine territory.

The Israelites' wealth and well-being
were in the hands
of the very enemies they were trying to fight.

And if that was not enough,
the Ark of the Covenant was missing,
because the Philistines felt to take it.

It was a losing battle,
but a heart aflame will set cities alight.

A teenage shepherd boy stood quietly in secluded forests.
Unpopular in every aspect,

but nonetheless, he saw the depravity of his nation,
and had a heart to bring it back to its rightful place.

I wonder if he knew that looking after sheep
would prepare him to lead the flock of Israel.

I wonder if he knew that slaying a Philistine giant
would make him a king amongst the people.

I wonder if he knew his musical experimentation
would bring about artistic revival.

I wonder if he knew that his heart aflame
would set cities alight.

His name was David,
and his aim was clear:
to explore and express the heart of God.

And through his love for music,
David achieved this unlike any other.
His musicianship carried divine power,
so much so that when his hand touched the strings,
and his mind was set on the Divine Creator,
he could drive demons out of the very hearts of men.
Read 1 Samuel 16:14-23.

David was the first to integrate music into everyday worship.
His efforts can now be found in nearly every worship service.
Scripture mentions music the most during David's time.
He was the trigger for what we can call The Hebrew Renaissance.

His lyrical content was so transparent
it still continues to touch hearers.

He wrote most of the 'Book of Psalms': his heart 'spilt in song'.

The book itself was essentially split into five separate books:

BOOK I
Psalm 1-41

BOOK II
Psalm 42-72

BOOK III
Psalm 73-89

BOOK IV:
Psalm 90-106

BOOK V:
Psalm 107-150

Why five separate books?
The final editors of the Psalms marvelled at its variety,
and thought it to be compared
to the five books of the Torah,
the law of God.

The Hebrews saw the Psalms as tutorials,
the poetical commandments on reaching the heart of God.
It explored every emotion,
dissected every circumstance.
Essentially, it was a full and complete soundtrack to life.

His name was David.
A king with a skip in his step,
and he was the only one dancing,
until the day he decided to do what the other kings avoided,
and fearlessly marched into Philistine camps,
slaying every man found,
bringing the Ark of the Covenant back into the city.

The presence of God is back in the city.
Now, the entire nation is dancing.

And David was not finished.
He wanted to build another place for the Ark to reside,
but he did not want to create another tabernacle.

Tabernacles were portable,
and were needed for a people who were searching for a home,
but the people are now established.
David sought to build a temple,
brick and cement.
An immoveable building.
A permanent home for God.

God was intrigued by the request,
and even loved the idea of David building the temple,
but the truth remained,
the temple could not be built with bloody hands,
and David, by reputation, was a man of war.

So God moved to Plan B,
and gave the duty of building the temple to David's son.
His son was named Solomon.

Still,
that never stopped David from preparing resources.
He provided the materials needed to build,
he delegated roles to the priesthood,
he selected the musicians,
he wrote the songs for a temple

that was not even under construction yet,
he offered finances for upkeep,
he even drew up the blueprints of the temple,
of which he said in 1 Chronicles 28:19,
"the LORD made me *understand in writing, by His hand upon me,*
all the works of these plans."

God made a musician a fully qualified architect.

Godly inspiration drove him to even greater lengths.
Amos 6:5 shows that David was an explorer of sounds.
He invented for himself instruments that would
expand his musical language.
He made these instruments in their thousands.

Four thousand to be exact,
according to 1 Chronicles 23:5.

Let us just say these were all stringed instruments:
harps, for example.

If David was in our modern day,
and he was expected to craft the same amount of harps,
all by himself,
David would not leave his workshop,
until one thousand three hundred & thirty three years later;
without tea breaks.

He worked furiously,
he worked relentlessly,
and above all,
he worked passionately.

His dedication established a key lesson:
not even a king is too busy to do the work of the Lord.

His investments into the arts were plenteous,
bringing the city from having no blacksmiths,
to being full to the brim with craftsmen,
storytellers,
educators,
poets,
and musicians.

An entire generation of creatives
were birthed from this one man.
A heart aflame *can* set cities alight.
And David,
being one of the greatest kings the land has ever seen,
reached a ripe old age.
And after successfully seeing his city ablaze,
he had no more fire to give.

So he laid his head to rest,
and fell into a sleep,
until his fire simply burnt out.

CHAPTER FIVE

BREADTH OF MIND

THE THREE PROPERTIES OF GOD'S CREATIVITY

God moved to Plan B,
and gave the duty of building the temple to David's son.
His son was named Solomon.

And knowing Solomon had big shoes to fill,
God appeared to him one night in a dream,
offering Solomon his heart's desires.

In those few moments of dreamtime,
Solomon could have asked for anything.
A little bit of fame,
a little bit of fortune,
a little more life,
a little less war.

But Solomon did one better, and asked for wisdom.
To have a heart that is able to lead such a great city.

God paused for a moment,
then applauded him.
He gave what Solomon asked,
plus all of the trimmings.

And this explains
why Solomon's bank account was so incredible.
1 Kings 10:27 states that he made silver to be like stones.
Anything below gold was tarmac.
If it was not twenty-four carat,
it was not in Solomon's house.

David spent his life in war.
Not Solomon.
From the time of his reign to the time of his death,
Solomon slept cosy.

But all of that was dust compared to Solomon's first request
'And God gave Solomon wisdom
and exceedingly great understanding,
and largeness of heart like the sand on the seashore' *1 Kings 4:29*

The wisdom of men
and the wisdom of God are not to be compared.
God is wise enough to make planets,
men are only wise enough to discover them.

Solomon was filled with the wisdom of God.
Rich in mind, and that made him the richest man of all.

When your wisdom comes from God,
three properties reside...

NO. 1
ABUNDANCE

1 Kings 4:29 says that Solomon was given "largeness of heart". We can call it 'breadth of mind'. He had a taste to explore and discover the known universe. He was filled with strong curiosity, and this curiosity drove him to understand nature, physics, biology, sociology, and all kinds of artistry. There was not a thing on earth he did not explore. 1 Kings 4:32 says that he wrote three thousand proverbs and one thousand and five songs; that is around eighty-three albums worth of material.

When your wisdom comes from God,
your well will never dry.

NO. 2
DOMINANCE

The intellectuals of the east, the inventors of ancient Egypt, and the queen of Sheba. All of these people were masterminds in their own right, but 1 Kings 4:34 says that all the kings of the globe travelled far and wide to hear the wisdom of Solomon. 1 Kings 10:23 states that Solomon's riches and wisdom surpassed them all.

When your wisdom comes from God,
kings and princes will confide.

NO. 3
LONGEVITY

We still have the book of Proverbs, we still have the book of Ecclesiastes and we still have the Songs Of Solomon. Like his father David, Solomon's writings are still used for teaching, thousands of years after his death.

When your wisdom comes from God,
your words will never die.

After seven years of labour,
the temple reached completion.

And it was beautiful.

Gold-plated walls.
Gold-plated floors.
It was the joy of the city,
and a statement to the world:

God has a home,
and His home is in Jerusalem.

God looked at the finished product and was pleased

…ish

Temples and tabernacles were beautiful gestures,
and God was happy to dwell with His people,
but this was not exactly what God had in mind for a
'happily ever after'.
The gap between man and God was still apparent.
After all, God is omnipresent,
He is everywhere,
yet His only invitation to inhabit earth
was in a small building in Jerusalem.
It was cute,
but it was too exclusive.
Too restricting.
God needed to get closer.
God needed to fill the earth.

And residing inside of Him was an idea most controversial,
a Master-plan.
And He sought to fulfil this Master-plan
through a special individual.

'The Spirit of the LORD shall rest upon Him,
The Spirit of wisdom and understanding,
The Spirit of counsel and might,
The Spirit of knowledge
and of the fear of the LORD' *Isaiah 11:2*

The skill of Bezalel,
the heart of David,
the wisdom of Solomon,
combined into one.

A man that will finally bridge the gap.

Once again, God smiled to Himself,
as He thinks to do The Unthinkable.

CHAPTER SIX

SEVENTY-TWO HOURS

THE DEFINITION OF SUCCESS

In the silence, a command was given.
"LET THERE BE LIGHT".

0000:000:00:00:01

And from that moment onwards,
the Master-plan was underway.
The temples,
the tabernacles,
the prophecies,
they were all setting the stage,
for this one instant in history.

A man stripped naked
with flaps of His own flesh hanging off His body.
A King
with a crown of thorns on His head.

The All Knowing One
who planted the seed,
which grew to be a tree,
which was axed down to the ground,
to become the cross He was stapled to.

He knew the craftsman
who made the nails,
that are now pressed into His hands and feet.

He read the thoughts
of the Roman soldiers,
who publicly beat Him half to death.

He knew the resting place
of the shoes that once ran to Him,
and are now hidden from Him.

He was aware of all of this,
yet He considers it all to be a successful conclusion to a life.

He looks up to the sky with a glimmer in His eyes,
a sigh of relief,
and a sense of accomplishment.

This is Jesus of Nazareth, King of the Jews.

He healed the sick,
He raised the dead,
He comforted the broken-hearted,
He changed the world.

David taught with song.
Solomon taught with riddles.
Jesus taught with stories.

And Jesus was full of them.
Mark 4:34 says He refused to speak to anybody
without telling a tale.

Why stories?
Because Jesus understood something crucial about them;
storytelling is one of the few methods that reach
the inner core of a person.

The Kingdom of Heaven is like a man with one hundred sheep.
One of the sheep goes missing.
The Shepherd forsakes the ninety-nine to find the one lost sheep.
We are the lost sheep.
God is looking for His people.
Let Him find you.

He took the complexity of God's authority,
and made it so relatable that little children understood it.

He walked from city to city,
telling the people about the new government approaching,
a government where man and God will rule alongside on earth,
just like the good old days.

He spoke about

THE KINGDOM.

The King's dominion.
A new culture.
A new way of thinking.

A rulership that would liberate the people
instead of holding them captive.
A rulership in which Jesus would be King.

But not all of His words were sweet to the ears.
Some of His sayings sickened many.

He once stood before the temple,
and in front of respectable religious leaders said:
"tear this whole place down
and I will rebuild it in three days".

The religious leaders were enraged beyond belief.
And now, Jesus hangs on a cross,
gathering just enough strength to gasp for air.

Yet this is all part of the Plan.
This was all a success.

For man was once the self-portrait of God,
until the acidic nature of sin was thrown onto the canvas,
altering the entire appearance of the Masterpiece.

The malfunction infuriated God,
seeing His artistic efforts go to waste.
All of His time,
all of His love,
all for nothing.

And what does an artist do to an art piece that is beyond repair?
He destroys it.

From that moment on,
we were irreversible failures.
Men with expiry dates,
just living life to die in a furnace of unquenchable fire.

But then The Unthinkable happened.

God just could not bring Himself to destroy us.
He became so engrossed by His art,
that He sought to *become* His art.
Merging two of His greatest ideas together:
the body,
and the temple.

He formed His new idea in the womb of a virgin,
A clean vessel that would birth the Saviour of the world,
Jesus, the perfect art piece.

God in the flesh.
He dwelt among us,
yet we would not recognise Him if he passed us on the street.

He looked like us,
walked like us,
laughed like us,
just so He could talk with us,
live with us,
die for us.

His body was
THE OUTER COURT
The place where He interacted with the outside world

His soul was
THE INNER COURT
The place where He sacrificed selfish ambition and pride

His Spirit was
THE HOLY OF HOLIES
The place where the God of this universe claimed residence

He spoke about destroying a temple.
He spoke about Himself.

His body was the temple.

He hung on the cross,
and *all* of the furious frustration of God,
formerly reserved for mankind,
was poured out fully on Jesus.

He smiles as He takes our place.

And now the prophecy in Isaiah 53:10 is brought to clarity;
where it says it pleased the Father to bruise the Son.

God vented His anger on His Masterpiece,
so when He looks at us,
the disfigured work of art,
He looks at us with fresh eyes,
with all fury vaporised,
and makes efforts to mould us back into His image.

Back to our original state,
as if nothing happened.

"IT
IS
FINISHED" Jesus cries.
The Master-plan is complete.
He bows His head as the crowd cheers.

Christ's crucifixion: the definition of success.

Seventy-two hours later,
He steps out of His own grave,
with His temple rebuilt,
and pats Himself on the back for a job well done.

All differences have been settled.
Man can now be at peace with God.
The Kingdom on earth can now be established.

CHAPTER SEVEN

JESUS TIMES TWO

THE ARCHITECTURE OF THE CHURCH

What is The Church?
What did Jesus visualise when He bled and died for it?

Much more than mere religion.
Much more than brick and cement.

Think of RUACH,
the Spirit of God.
In times past, God's Spirit would come upon a select few.
And these individuals,
even though one or two,
would influence entire generations.

It descended upon Bezalel,
and he crafted the first earthly home for God.

It enflamed David,
and he set a city alight.

It inspired Solomon,
and he wrote the wisest words the world has ever witnessed.

It rested in the heart of Jesus,
and He saved the world.

The Spirit only moved in the lives of a select few.
But 33 A.D changed all of that.

Shortly after the resurrection of Jesus,
an age-old prophecy was being unveiled before the people.

Acts 2 tell us that in an upper room,
on the day of Pentecost,
one hundred and twenty people were filled with RUACH.

Joel 2:28's promise was fulfilled.
God said that in the last days,
He would pour out His Spirit upon ALL flesh.

RUACH, now known as the Holy Spirit,
fell upon the hearts of believing men,
and has set hearts aflame ever since.

The Spirit,
which only displayed its full power in The Holy Of Holies,
is now abiding in the bodies of men.

The same Spirit that empowered Jesus,
is now the Spirit that empowers us.

So even if you and I
were the only ones on the planet filled with His Spirit,
we are Jesus times two.

We are double,
triple,
even quadruple the force Jesus was.
That is why He told His disciples
"he who believes in Me, the works that I do he will do also;
and greater works than these he will do" *John 14:12*

No longer does God need to inhabit one temple at a time,
we are all now walking tabernacles.
He could inhabit millions simultaneously.

Acts 1:8 says it best:
the Holy Spirit is POWER
and makes us a WITNESS that God exists.

And if we carry this power individually,
what will happen if we come together collectively?

'Arise, shine; for your light has come!
And the glory of the LORD is risen upon you.
For behold, the darkness shall cover the earth,
and deep darkness the people;
but the LORD will arise over you,
and His glory will be seen upon you.

The Gentiles shall come to your light,
and kings to the brightness of your rising' *Isaiah 60:1-3*

Time and time again,
God has used the creative thinker and the artist
to build bridges between God and man.

Now, we reach an age where the world is at its darkest,
and our generation needs God's love
demonstrated to them in a new way.

We will have the ideas
that would bring them out of their poverty.

New businesses need to be launched.
New books need to be written.
New medicines need to be discovered.
New ministries need to be initiated.

The world needs newness.
The world needs creativity.

Remember BARA.
Fresh supplies of creativity can only be sourced from God.
And if we believe to be connected to the only creative source,
then true innovation should really come from us.

What would happen if we unlock
this creative power invested in us?
How bright would our lights shine?

Do you want to know what The Church is?
Do you want to know what Jesus visualised
when He bled and died for it?

The Church is the lighthouse.
It is the sum of every person who believes in Him,
irrespective of race,
family background,

financial history,
educational status.

Spiritual liberation is no longer exclusive for the Israelites.
We are all now the spiritual Israelites of the world.
We carry His wealth and wisdom.
We are the visual representatives of the King on earth.

The Church is the body of Christ.
Our faith in Jesus is the flesh that links the body,
and we are all made alive by the blood of Jesus.
His blood circulates throughout the body,
and connects its members to the heart and mind of God.

We are the body,
Christ is the head.
We move according to how He thinks.
That is what it means to be Kingdom-minded.

Establishing God's Kingdom on earth is our duty.
So with the divine power invested in us,
we will generate works of art with every tool and talent we have,
until we effectively reintroduce this culture to Jesus.

God said "LET THERE BE LIGHT",
And now here we are.

In tribute, we will continue to shine.
We will keep the fire burning
with every ounce of energy we have,
until the hands of the clock reaches its last second,
and it all goes back down to zero.

0000:000:00:00:00

VOLUME II

PHOS

THE LIGHT OF THE CULTURE

CHAPTER ONE

INDESTRUCTIBLE

THE SMARTEST KIDS IN BABYLON

INSPIRED BY THE BOOK OF DANIEL

There is a term for such a person
who is young enough to understand a culture,
but is Godly enough to be untouched by it.

Welcome to Babylon,
where men are the gods of the land,
and the scent of sin is heavy in the air.

The home of the immoral,
the land of the loose.
The place where anything goes,
and everything is up for grabs:
sex,
money,
entertainment.
It is all here,
and it is all yours.
Indulge yourself in this sin-infested circus.

Jerusalem is in ruins.
Jerusalem is bare.
And all of the Israelites
walk into this strange city in shackles and chains;
slaves to the new world power.

Babylon,
the most degrading
yet most imaginatively innovative city on the planet.

And on the throne of this empire
was a king called Nebuchadnezzar.

Nebuchadnezzar,
like most kings,
desired world domination.

His goal was to seize every nation,
and magnetise every individual,
until eventually, the entire globe would think,

eat and sleep like a Babylonian.

There was no room for other cultures to infiltrate,
including the seemingly restricting culture of the Israelites.

Babylon danced before multiple gods,
Israel only served one.
Babylon required you to live the laws of the land,
but Israel would only follow the laws of God.

Nebuchadnezzar did not like this at all.

Hebrew culture failed to fall in sync
with the rest of the world's beliefs.
So the king decided to eradicate their belief system completely.

Out of the Jewish slaves,
Nebuchadnezzar picked out a small group of boys,
All between the ages of eleven and nineteen.
Well taught,
highly intelligent,
widely recognised in the Jewish community,
and kids who carried celebrity quality.

Nebuchadnezzar would free their ankles from shackles,
and cloak them with a robe of royalty.
He would feed them,
pamper them,
grant them scholarship in Babylon's greatest university,
and rank them as a high member in Babylonian society.

Knowing that Israelites put
great importance on the names of their children,
and deemed a name as a calling and purpose of a child,
Nebuchadnezzar would change their names entirely,
making their callings no longer tributes to the God of Israel,
but to the gods of the culture.

~~**DANIEL**~~
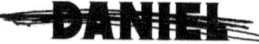
(God is my judge)

is now **BELTESHAZZAR**
(Bel will protect)

~~**HANANIAH**~~
~~(Jehovah is gracious)~~

is now **SHADRACK**
(Servant of Aku)

~~**MISHAEL**~~
~~(Who is like God?)~~

is now **MESHACH**
(Who is like Aku?)

~~**AZARIAH**~~
~~(Jehovah helps)~~

is now **ABEDNEGO**
(Servant of Nebo)

The boys would then be ripe for manipulation.
After three years of heavy indoctrination,
the boys will become Babylonian men.
Returning to their Jewish relatives,
they would poison the people with Babylonian thinking,
Until after a time,
all Hebrew culture would be totally forgotten.

The plan was foolproof.
Young people lead young people.

But out of these young people,
four boys saw right through it all.
Daniel, Shadrack, Meshach, and Abednego.

Their names were changed,
but their mission was never forgotten:
to draw God's people out of bondage
by all means necessary.

They resembled the rest of the students,
but in the night times, God would visit them in dreams,
showing them visions of political advancements;
global events that were yet to occur.

The Spirit of God was so strong in them,
that after three years of study,
when compared to all of the magicians,
and all of the astrologers,
the four boys were found
ten times smarter than every one of them.

Thus, pushing them to the top of their class,
and making them the smartest kids in Babylon.

Nebuchadnezzar was taken aback by their intellect,
but Daniel caught the king's eye especially.

He became so fascinated by Daniel's spiritual insight,
that he began to share his personal dreams with the boy.
Daniel decoded each and every dream with ease.
Nebuchadnezzar saw use for Daniel,
and made him a powerful man in Babylon.
The head of the university,
and ruler of a portion of the empire.

Daniel brought his three friends along with him,
and put them all in high positions.
Shadrack, Meshach, and Abednego became governors of the city.
All was well.

The day then occurred
when Nebuchadnezzar beheld himself in a mirror,
and felt he required more worship from the people.

He built himself a statue.
All solid gold.
All in his image.
He assembled the entertainment.
He rounded up the orchestra.
He invited swarms of people
to attend the biggest self-worship service Babylon had ever seen.

When the people gathered in their herds,
a command was given,
and the command was straightforward:

"The moment you hear the music play,
fall down to your knees,
and bow down to the statue, which I have made."

And the moment the beat dropped,
the people worshipped.
To the left,

to the right,
behind,
and before.

Everyman,
from every creed,
and every tongue,
fell down to worship this god of Babylon.

Everyone,
minus three.

Shadrach,
Meshach,
Abednego.

Their promotion,
their fame,
their riches,
were forsaken in a heartbeat.

Many would have felt indebted to Nebuchadnezzar,
but these three could not allow the perks of a culture
compromise their faith.
And they were willing to publicly denounce it all,
just to make a statement:

God is the real King,
and we will bow to no other.

What disrespect.

Nebuchadnezzar stormed through the crowd,
hoping his newly-employed governors suddenly
gained arthritis in the knees.

He lovingly reassured them of his authority,
and then threatened to kill them all.

But standing toe-to-toe with the king,
they plainly responded,
"we are not hesitant to answer back.
If you plan to kill us,
God will deliver us.
And if by chance He decides not to,
just know that today,
three people did not bow down to you."

They left the king no choice.

The three boys were thrown into a furnace of intense heat
with fire so severe it scorched the men who threw them in.

The three boys were thrown into the furnace,
but there were no screams to be heard.
No cries for help.

The king out of curiosity looked to see the burning,
and saw not three,
but four people in the furnace.

One resembling the Son of God.

The three boys walked out of the furnace
with every single thread of their clothing intact.
Completely unharmed.

There is a term for such a person
who is young enough to understand a culture,
but is godly enough to be untouched by it…

…Indestructible.

Whether it is a wall of wood, brick or steel,
you pierce through them all.
Nothing is able to stop you.

He was just a slave boy,
now Daniel is the vice president of Babylon.
The culture's intention for him was to be a young celebrity,
destroying the spiritual foundations of the nations.
But God's plan prevailed,
and now Daniel uses his platform
to show the people their true identity.

A mission accomplished without a single compromise.

Out of a godless culture,
arose a Godly influence.

'But the people who know their God shall be strong, and carry
out great exploits. And those of the people who understand shall
instruct many' *Daniel 11:32-33*

We will be the Indestructibles…
…the Daniels of this generation.

CHAPTER TWO

GODLESS

'...The world is crucified to me,
and I to the world' *Galatians 6:14*

In all your creative expressions,
remember this:
They hung your King to a cross,
so expect no better treatment.

Expect giggling,
for you are the clowns of the culture.
Expect chuckles,
for you are the laughing stocks of the world.

'...We have been made a spectacle unto the world,
and to angels and to men.
We are fools for Christ's sake'
1 Corinthians 4:9-10

As the beliefs of a fragile culture shift,
the word of God remains unchangeable.
So we will continue to look weird and out of place
as the world cries el oh el.

I could tell you about the origins of Christian art,
but there is little to say for the most part.
The first three hundred years would go unaccounted for;
back when Christianity was an illegal practice.

We had no mega churches or celebrity preachers,
but we were thrown in coliseums,
and eighty thousand spectators would roar with an applause,
as we were ripped to shreds by lions.

We never sung 'This little light of mine'
but we were soaked in oil,
and we were lit on fire,
to be the burning street lamps of Rome.

If you seek to know the origins of Christian art,

there is little you will find,
for the only paint we used to articulate our faith with,
was our blood splashed on Roman walls.

And yet it spoke volumes.
Christianity grew stronger by the generation.

Rome fell,
and the Middle Ages arose.

Christianity went from a poor man's religion,
to a state power.

And after finally gaining freedom to express our faith without fear,
we saw fit to invent new ways to communicate the gospel.

In a world filled with illiterate folk,
we extensively taught with visuals,
making the church the number one financers of the arts.

We adopted drama in its earliest form,
and created the mystery plays.
We took the scriptures to the streets,
exploring all kinds of special effects,
set designs and writing styles
with plays running up to twenty hours,
lasting a number of days.

We gained an exquisite taste in architecture.
We made sure everything
from the stained glass windows,
to the organ pipes,
to the very furniture had Christian theology woven into its detail.

We were humble artists
who never saw ourselves as 'the elite few',
but artists with a message to share;
hardly signing our own paintings after completion.

The church was the leading force in the arts industry.
We were the articulators of the truth.
But then corruption and perversion crept in.
The art became the gospel's replacement.

The artefacts that were used to aid prayer,
were now being prayed to.

The paintings that were supposed to reach the lost,
went from being three dimensional and realistic,
to flat and symbolic.

Jesus no longer looked like an approachable saviour,
but a distant judge.

The paintings of the saints no longer resembled everyday people,
but glorified icons.

Christian teaching became so spiritual and other-worldly,
that the general public could no longer
relate to anything religious.
Men distorted Christianity.
The church was no longer a loving community
but a controlling one,
alienating outsiders.

Hence, man's great distaste for religion surfaces.
And here is birthed the arrival of two movements:

The first – *The Renaissance*
The people of Florence saw religion as restriction,
and never again wanted to be associated
with the idea of an all-powerful God.
Man would now be the source of all power and authority.

This philosophy caused an awakening in society,
and a rebirth of what men thought of themselves.

Humanism:
Where the term 'Genius'
once used to describe an unknown guiding spirit
leading an artist to excellence,
was now used to name the artists themselves.
Humanistic thought was growing rapidly,
and art was used as the primary tool to push its message forward.

Artistic quality regenerated,
literature flourished,
education thrived,
egos were encouraged.

Self-portraits became an officially recognised form of art.
Men began to sign their own works.
Artists became more desired than the paintings they painted.
Artists went from being humble mortals,
to being the gods of society.

The second movement – *The Reformation*
The church grew sick of distorted Christianity,
and desired spiritual rehabilitation.
No more unbiblical religious activities.
No more financial greed and corruption.
No more false teaching.
Sola Scriptura:
Scripture Only.

The leading men of this revolt saw no issue with art per se.
Art was deemed an effective tool,
as long as it never distracted from the gospel of Jesus.
But the enraged followers took no prisoners,
and no longer saw need for the arts,
destroying every scrap of art they could find.

Cathedrals were burnt down to the ground.
Stained glass windows where smashed.
Paintings were ripped apart.

The church renounced all arts.
Music scarcely survived.

The first movement was godless,
the second was Godly.

The first movement used art to further their beliefs.
The second forsook the arts completely.

The first movement grew stronger century by century,
and infested all arts and education with humanist beliefs.
And for a time, the society felt free from the constraints of God.
But like most sin,
it liberates,
then drains,
then kills.

Schools begin to educate children on the non-existence of God.
When these children finally ask the big question
'how did we get here?'
They are shown the monkey.

They are taught that they are nothing but atomic mass,
and the design of this universe is all by coincidence,
and nothing was by intent,
including their very lives.

They are taught this until the twinkle in their eye dulls to black.

Lively children leave education as lifeless robots.

The anthem resounds:

NO GOD.
NO MEANING.
NO PURPOSE BUT DEATH.
THOUGHTS OF UNFULFILLMENT?
IGNORE AND SUPPRESS.

NO GOD.
NO MEANING.
NO PURPOSE BUT DEATH.
THOUGHTS OF UNFULFILLMENT?
IGNORE AND SUPPRESS.

This anthem affects the things we watch,
the music we listen to,
the clothes we wear.

Shaping how we view our world,
shaping how we view ourselves.

And the people,
with this message of hopelessness pumped into them,
live day in and day out without motive.
Men filled with unfulfillment,
hoping to find salvation in shot glasses and antidepressants.

The nations remain godless,
when believers proclaim God less.

We went from mystery plays and architectural ventures,
to tracts and t-shirts.

We would prefer to write songs
that are more current than anointed.
Always singing about God,
yet never saying Jesus.

The world's spiritual virtue is at an all time low,
and it is up to us,
the second movement,
to be revived in our creative efforts,
and bring about the real renaissance.
A true rebirth in culture.

But expect giggling,
because you are expected to express the words of God
in an atheistic society.
Expect chuckles,
for the gospel you express will always fail to make logical sense.

No matter how beautifully you articulate God's Word,
you will always look alien,
you will always look old-fashioned,
you will always seem extreme.

You know it,
I know it,
God knows it.

It will never sound right to the ear,
and God would not have it any other way.

He calls it the 'foolishness of preaching' in 1 Corinthians 1:25,
but then says in the eighteenth verse:
'it is to them that perish foolishness, but for us it is power'.
God summons petty things, like our artistic skill,
and empowers them to save souls.

So in all of your creative expressions,
understand this:
your creativity by itself is incapable of saving a single soul.
No fleshy attempt can fulfil such an impossible task.

You cannot by mere song or design convince anybody to love God.
Only the power of God carries that ability.

Unless the power of God backs you,
your evangelistic attempts are pointless.

'The Kingdom is not in word, but in power' *1 Corinthians 4:20*

1 Corinthians 9:16-18 says it plainly:
if we do express the gospel willingly,
we will lose popularity,
we will even be made outcasts,
BUT a reward will await us.
If we fail to communicate God to this culture,
we will keep friends,
we will remain popular,
BUT we will face the hard consequences of our compromise.

Either way, it is a tough decision,
but to those who seek to creatively express the gospel,
our reward is this:
to know that we have hold of a mystery.
And this mystery has been hidden from the earth
for thousands of years.
It is a mystery that is able to secure an individual's eternity.

And we are able to take this *very same* mystery,
and reveal it to *whosoever* we please.

The priceless knowledge of God,
distributed free of charge.

We give men access to God.
That is our reward.

And our mission is vast,
1 Timothy 2:3-4 tells us that God desires
to have the gospel accessible to all.
Our creative expressions must reach everybody,
from the hobo to the celebrity.

Our duty to live Christian lives
in a godless culture is a costly one.
But to know that the message inside of us
can bring millions of corpses to life…
…It is worth all the chuckles in the world.

CHAPTER THREE

FULLNESS OF TIME

'Go into all the world and preach the gospel to every creature'
Mark 16:15

It is God's responsibility to save souls,
it is our responsibility to give souls access to Him.

Jesus came to earth with perfect timing.
Not a day earlier,
not a day later.
Galatians 4:4 calls it the 'fullness of time'.

It is 33 A.D,
and Jesus tells His disciples to preach to every creature.

It is 33 A.D,
and Roman roads are paved all over the globe,
making the spreading of the gospel easier than ever.

It is 46 A.D,
and Paul is adopting Roman technology
to reach fifty percent of the Roman Empire.

It is 1454,
and knowledge is reserved solely for the proud and wealthy.
Manuscripts are handwritten by monks in dungeons.
It is 1454,
and the poor can only dream of reading a book.
But then came 1455,
when Johannes Gutenberg invented the printing press.
Fast, clean, efficient.
Books can now be made in moments.
Knowledge can now be distributed to the masses.

It is 1455,
and Gutenberg seeks to create the world's first printed book.
A printed book that would be a statement to society,
and a body of words that should always be at the forefront of
technology.

It is 1455,
and The Bible is the first book to be printed.
It is the 2000s,
and The Bible is the best-selling book in history.

It is 1825,
and an artist named Samuel Morse
reads about the death of his wife.
Even though her body is three hundred miles away,
Samuel Morse could have made it to the funeral,
if the letter had not taken more than a week to reach him.

It is 1832,
and Samuel Morse,
being a victim of slow communication,
wonders if messages could be sent from
one person to another in an instant.
He experiments with electrical impulses,
and after many years of trial and error,
he finds the solution.

It is May 24th 1844,
and Samuel Morse has invented the telegraph,
stretching its wires from Washington to Baltimore.
He publicly tests his invention,
making sure the first message sent through telegraph wires,
was an earth-shattering statement;
one that would make the world know the source
of Morse's inspiration:

'WHAT HATH GOD WROUGHT?'

It is May 24th 1844,
and the first message sent through telegraph wires,
has initiated the summoning of all modern communications.

Out of the telegraph, came the radio in 1855.

1923 introduced S. Parkes Cadman,

the first man to use the radio for evangelism,
reaching five million American souls in just five years.

It is 1923,
and Aimee McPherson has built the world's first megachurch
known as Angelus Temple.
She used plays to illustrate sermons almost every week,
and harnessed the power of advertising
with attention-grabbing billboards,
bringing the unapologetic truth of the gospel to Hollywood.

It is April 14th 1952,
and TIME magazine coins the term 'televangelist'
for a man named Fulton J Sheen,
the first believer to preach on television sets.
His show was named 'Life Worth Living',
a programme expected to gain minimum interest,
but ended up grabbing thirty million viewers a week;
eventually winning an Oscar in the long run.

It is 2011,
and Twitter is looking for their most influential users,
and stare at their statistics in utter confusion,
as they find the tweets of T.D. Jakes and Joyce Meyer
more influential than those of Justin Beiber and Lady Gaga.

Innovation upon innovation.
No matter what the technology,
God's word will forever remain strong.

And as technology cheapens by the decade,
earth-shaking devices can now be found
in the hands of the poor and rich.

Now anyone has the ability to change the world.
All the technology you need is right in your pocket.

God will continue to encourage innovation,
until His gospel is accessible to everyone.
The fullness of time has come upon us,
and the gospel needs to be expressed in new inventive ways.

It is now our turn to adopt the necessary technologies,
and make the good news accessible to every creature.

CHAPTER FOUR

SALT & LIGHT

Read Matthew 5-7.
Jesus preached a sermon about you.
His excitement drove Him to tell it on a mountain.

Read Matthew 5:13.
He called you the salt of the earth.
You preserve a culture.
You bring out the best flavours in society.

You are the salt of the earth.
And salt,
in those days,
was essential to the world's economy.
Roman soldiers' wages were paid in salt.

You are the salt of the earth.
You create the jobs,
you make the inventions,
you have the ideas that boost money back into the economy.

Read Matthew 5:14-16.
He called you the light of the world.

Light is speed.
Light is the fastest speed in the known universe.
Speed is innovation.
Your creativity is light-years ahead.

Moses saw the Light,
and witnessed the beginning of time,
writing Genesis in the process.

John saw the Light,
and witnessed the end of time,
writing Revelation in the process.

Paul saw the Light,
and witnessed things so advanced,
Jesus told him never to write them down.

You have the quickest access to heaven through God,
and God has the quickest access to earth through you.

God is the inventor of everything,
all ideas come from Him,
but you are the light,
and He wants to birth His best ideas through you.

You will create genres of music the world has never heard before,
design clothes the world has never worn before,
teach things the world has never learnt before.

The world moves fast,
very fast,
but you move faster.

You are timeless.

He preached a sermon about you,
and He called you the light of the world.

The Greek word for light is

PHOS.

PHOS,
means light,
but it is the light of the Sun.

You are the Sun of the world.
You are blindingly noticeable.
You illuminate the entire planet.
You are the earth's main source of energy.

Your brightness catches the attention of many,
but never hide it.
We need it.

'Let your light so shine before men, that they may *see* your good
works and *glorify your Father in heaven*' Matthew 5:16

Jesus preached a sermon about you,
and He called you salt and light,
the economy and innovation of the planet.

CHAPTER FIVE

UNLEARN EVERYTHING

'But as it is written,
"Eye has not seen,
nor ear heard,
nor have entered into the heart of man
the things which God hath prepared for those who love Him."
But God has revealed them unto us through His Spirit.
For the Spirit searches all things,
yes, the deep things of God' *1 Corinthians 2:9-10*

Our doctorates,
our degrees,
our intelligence,
is of little use here.

The deepness of the ocean
is the shallowness of God.
The wisdom of men
is the stupidity of God.

A hundred billion stars in the galaxy,
and a hundred billion galaxies in the universe,
yet God knows you by name,
and wishes to teach you a thing or two.

In John 14:26, Jesus gave us a promise,
and His promise spoke about the Holy Spirit dwelling in us,
and becoming our *teacher.*

Not only would the Spirit teach,
but scripture says it would teach us *all* things.

1 John 2:27 says that no man needs to teach us anything,
for our tutor is the Omniscient One.

Omniscient,
all knowledge.

Think of a subject,
the Spirit can teach it.

So if you are creative,
which you are,
congratulations,
you have access to inexhaustible innovation.
You have potential to be the most inventive mortal on the planet,
all because you are connected to the most creative supply.

And that is why we could never be
jealous of another man's intellect.
We have enrolled into the best university
in the universe.

But to move past our earthly wisdom,
and to be educated in the wisdom of God,
one thing is required from you before enrolment:

Unlearn everything.

Forget everything you think you know
about life,
about creativity,
everything.

'Let no one deceive himself. If anyone among you seems to be wise
in this age, let him become a fool that he may become wise'
1 Corinthians 3:18

In Matthew 18:3-4
Jesus says a profound statement,
'Unless you are converted and become as little children,
you will by no means enter the Kingdom of Heaven'

Living a Christian life is incredibly simple,
but virtually impossible to live out with our stubborn adult minds.
It is completely against our human nature to live a Godly life.
That is why John 3 commands us to be *born again*.

And thus 2 Corinthians 5:17 makes perfect sense
when it calls us a 'new creation'.

An entirely new breed of human beings,
with a completely fresh way of thinking.

The Kingdom encourages childishness,
to think like a child,
and see the world with new eyes,
being full of curiosity and wonder.
When you do that,
you are able to solve the world's seemingly unsolvable problems.

The beautiful thing about God's creativity
is that it is completely *free*,
and He is willing to instruct anybody,
irrespective of educational background.

When Jesus picked the twelve men
He wanted to change the world,
He picked *highly uneducated* individuals,
including two fishermen named Peter and John.
But Acts 4:13 said that when the Spirit of God was on them,
and they opened their mouths,
those uneducated men spoke
with such knowledge and eloquence,
they shocked many.
The people deemed their intelligence
as *proof* that they had encountered Jesus.

The greatest wisdom
could be found in the most unsuspected individuals.

Knowledge that has been hidden from governors and kings,
is told to us plainly in our ears.

What could we create if we just opened up ourselves to God?

The body of Christ stands as a university
where anybody can thrive.

There are no prodigies or failures here.
There is no one who is more or less creative than the other,
only people who are more or less childish,
only people who are more or less
willing to open up themselves to God.

So knowing the power we have access to,
it should be every artist's duty and passion,
to take to time to know their Creator,
and through the Spirit,
explore the never-ending deepness of God.

ELEVEN TALENTS

The reality is this:
we are not the most innovative persons on the planet.
We serve a creative God,
but we are not as creative as He is.

There is a reason for this.
Matthew 25:14-30 explains:

Jesus tells us a story about a rich man.
This rich man gave his servants
a sum of money to do business with.
This sum of money is known as a 'talent'.

He gave one servant five talents,
he gave another two,
And he gave the last servant one.

The rich man went on his way.

The servant with five talents
did business and got five talents more.
The servant with two, two talents more.

The servant with one talent
was ashamed,
and dug a hole
to bury his talent in the ground.

The rich man comes back.

The servant with five talents more hears
"well done.
You have been faithful with little,
I will make you a ruler over much."

The second servant heard something similar.

The third servant got what was coming to him.

Have you ever heard of the Idea Currency Law?
Jesus is like the rich man.
And when He gives us ideas,
it is like giving us currency.

We are the servants,
stewards of His genius.
And it is a law,
that the more ideas you invest in,
the more ideas you earn.

God has embedded inventions, businesses,
and ministries inside of us.
The moment we begin to work on our first project,
God gives us ideas for the second.

That is God's way of saying,
"you have been faithful with the small ideas,
I will make you a ruler over bigger ones."

Creativity enriches you.
When we create,
we do not just make mere works of art,
but we open doors to people and places,
opportunities and finances.
We are able to access things
we would have never accessed otherwise,
if we failed to create.

The more you create,
the more you experience the boundless imagination of God.
The more you create,
the *freer* you become.

Some people have five ideas,
some have two,
but some of us just have one.

And some of us may feel our one idea is inadequate,

or our dreams are too big to pull off,
so we hide it under the rug,
hoping God never asks us about it again.
The rich man asks the servant with one talent about the money.
The servant admits to hiding it.
Read Matthew 25: 26 & 30.
The rich man calls him a "wicked and lazy servant".
One who should be thrown into "outer darkness",
where there is "weeping and gnashing of teeth".

I thought the rich man's response was a little dramatic,
to be honest.

But read Jesus' story in context.
He begins His speech in chapter 24,
where He tells us about the end of the world.

He talks about a darkness that would come,
that would be unlike any evil we have ever witnessed before.

War and famine,
sickness and sorrow.
He said that unless He shortens the days,
not a single human being on the planet will survive.
Situations on earth would be that horrific.

And then in the midst of all of that,
some of us did not feel inclined to use the one idea God gave us.

If each idea built the Kingdom,
we could not place at least one brick down?

That is why the rich man was furious.

When we fail to create, it is our poverty.
We rob ourselves,
we rob others,
we rob God.

In dark days like these,
the world must benefit from God's investment in you,
so do not be afraid to step out.

'Now to Him who is able to do exceedingly
abundantly above all that we ask or think,
according to the power that works in us' *Ephesians 3:20*

God exceeds our imagination.
He can supercede anything we ask of Him.

The dreams He gives us are never impossible to accomplish.
He gave us these ideas
because He believes we are able to flesh it out.
Some of us wonder why we struggle so much financially,
or why we go from day to day feeling so unfulfilled.
The answer is staring straight at you.

Your dreams,
pursue it.

It is more than a hobby,
it is a source of endless opportunity.
It is where most of your fulfilment and blessings will come from.

The rich man takes the one talent away from the servant,
and gives it to the servant with ten talents.

The man with ten talents now has eleven,
and is rich off another man's poverty.

Have you ever thought of an idea,
abandoned it,
then saw someone else get rich off the exact same idea years after?

Welcome to the Idea Currency Law.

The moral of the story is this,
God is gracious,
and He has invested much into us.
But now, we have no time to waste,
and must return the investment.

Live out your dreams,
or someone will live them out for you.

CHAPTER SEVEN

SKILL & WILL

Sometimes we would rather waste hours in front of screens,
than paint the sweetest picture the world has ever seen.

'The soul of a lazy man desires, and has nothing;
but the soul of the diligent shall be made rich' *Proverbs 13:4*

Let us not think that this is all one big spiritual experience,
where God downloads into us all artistic splendour,
and we involuntarily mould masterpieces
without any conscious efforts whatsoever.

Dreams remain dreams,
until you toil.

Are our notebooks empty?
Is there still much ink in our pens?
Have we invested in our craft?

For as much as God's power empowers us,
it can only thrive according to our skill and will.

Never forget skill.
Matthew 25:15 says that the rich man
gave every servant according to his ability.
The greater your ability,
the greater your responsibility.

If you sing mediocre,
God will not give you Madison Square Garden.
Talent is innate,
but greatness is worked towards.

So practice.
It is unavoidable.
Industry professionals do it,
you should even more.

When David was preparing for the temple,
and was gathering the ministers,

he chose two hundred and eighty-eight musicians.
1 Chronicles 25:7 states that he chose them because of their skill.

Industry standard is not enough,
whatever you create should exceed worldly benchmarks.

Your hard work plus God's power is a dangerous combination.
It will propel you to world-class status.

Daniel had a reputation in Babylon for his hard work.
Daniel 6:3 says he had a spirit of excellence inside of him.
It brought him from being slave boy
to vice president of the empire.

Can we strive for such excellence?

'Do you see a man who excels in his work? He will stand before
kings; he will not stand before unknown men' *Proverbs 22:29*

Worship is not limited to Sunday services.
Your work is your worship.
God's presence is not limited to tingly feelings.
Knowledge and enlightenment can be found in His presence.

Worship God before starting a project.
Ask for His presence to descend upon you.
Notice the shift in your idea generation,
As your creativity excites those around you.

Never forget skill,
yet never neglect will.

1 Chronicles 28:21 shows that in David's preparation,
he looked for craftsmen who were skilful,
but willing also.

David realised something we artists should all grasp:
the house of God needed to be made with love.

A warm dish served with a cold heart would never do.
God sees the works of a man's heart
as well as the works of a man's hands.
And David's heart was aflame.
'Surely I will not go into the chamber of my house,
or go up to the comfort of my bed;
I will not give sleep to my eyes or slumber to my eyelids,
until I find a place for the LORD' *Psalm 132:3-5*

His anxiety to see God's work completed
drove him to sleeplessness.
All-nighters focussed on God's work.

This reminds me of the classical composer Sebastian Bach,
who wrote twenty finished pages of music a day,
and a body of music ready for church every Sunday.
He did this while being a teacher of Latin,
a conductor,
a private instructor,
as well as being a father to twenty children.

Sebastian worked at great speed,
so much so that it took the Bach Gesellscaft
forty-six years to compile his work,
resulting in sixty thick volumes.

What drives a man to be so relentless in his work?
What gives a man such a willing heart to go the extra mile?
The answer is found in David's remarks to Solomon:
"..my son…the work is great,
because the temple is not for man,
but for the LORD God" *1 Chronicles 29:1*

Imagine the emperor of China,
or an African king,
or the president of the United States of America,
wanted you to create something for them.

Imagine they called you themselves,

and explained what they needed from you.
How would you react after you received the commission?
Would you produce work to the best of your ability?
Would you lose a few hours sleep to perfect the project?
Of course you would.
They are royalty,
and it is an honour to present your work before kings.

Well,
here is King Jesus,
nicknamed the King of kings.

The White House is child's play to Jesus.
The earth is His footstool.
And yet in all of His majesty,
He wants *you* to write that song.
He wants *you* to start that business.

You cannot get any better employment than that.

When you work for men, you should give a lot,
but when you work for the King of kings, you should give your all.

He deserves no less than the best art man can offer,
full stop.

The effort we put into our work
will show if we truly believe if Jesus is the real King or not.

Excellence is the standard.

Sometimes we would rather waste hours in front of screens,
than paint the sweetest picture the world has ever seen.

Take time out to perfect your craft.
Take time out to make artworks fit for a King.

CHAPTER EIGHT

MASCHIL

He hangs on a cross.
Gasping.

Roman soldiers gamble for His clothes.
Pedestrians walk by and smirk.
Friends are nowhere to be seen.

This is Jesus,
the man of sorrows.
In His loneliness,
He gathers enough strength to make a profound statement:
"Eli Eli lama sabacthani?"
which means
"My God, My God, why have You forsaken Me?"

Though He spoke it in Hebrew,
the spectators understood clearly what He meant.
Jesus was not making a statement for statements sake,
He was quoting a song.

A thousand years beforehand,
David writes Psalm 22,
a song of which he begins with the words
"My God, My God, why have You forsaken Me?"
The song then gives an account of a man
with pierced hands and feet,
who is ridiculed by the people,
and has His clothes confiscated and gambled.

David saw the crucifixion;
and wrote a song to document the entire event.

He was in the zone,
but intoxication was not his gateway to clarity.
David used no drug to get this kind of insight.
Instead, he disclosed his method for enlightenment
in Psalm 25:14:
'The secret of the LORD is with those who fear Him'

David's relationship with God was so intense,
that he was able to write songs about Jesus' death,
a thousand years before Jesus was born.
Christ admired David's inspired song writing so much,
that He paid tribute to it on the cross.
He then arose three days later,
telling the disciples in Luke 24:44
that all of the Psalms spoke about Him.

1 Chronicles 25:1 says that when David was choosing
musicians for the temple,
he needed skilful men,
but was more interested in men who prophesied with instruments.
They needed to allow God to shine through their craft.

Skill is good for the ear and is what men want,
prophecy is good for the soul and is what men need.
They were prophets first,
artists second.

Exodus 15:20-21 tells us about a song
a woman named Miriam sang,
when the Israelites escaped the hands of Egypt.
She is called a prophetess only *once* in scripture,
and that was in *this* instance.

We are not just artists,
we are prophets.
We express the heart of God.
He speaks to us and through us.

And if we are prophets,
then we cannot take our artistry lightly.
A great task is given to us as cultural caretakers.

If the eyes and ears are the gates to the soul,
then we must fulfil our role as gatekeepers.

'For Zion's sake I will not hold My peace,

and for Jerusalem's I will not rest,
until the righteousness goes forth as brightness,
and her salvation as a lamp that burns…
I have set watchmen on your walls, O Jerusalem;
they shall never hold their peace day or night.
You who make mention of the LORD, do not keep silent, and give Him no rest
till He establishes
and till He makes Jerusalem a praise in the earth'
Isaiah 62:1, 6-7

We are watchmen.
We must have an observant eye.
We must be sensitive to surrounding world events.
We must understand the people we reach.
We must be aware of their needs.
We must have foresight,
so we can prepare them for what lies ahead.

We must have artistic response-ability.
When troubles arise in the culture,
we are prophetic in our creative comebacks,
giving an answer to difficult questions.
Not just telling the future,
but proclaiming timely truth.

David spoke numerous times about singing a 'new song'.
The old songs were substantial,
but David always sought to keep it fresh.
So must we also continually create new works of art,
until Christ becomes famous in the culture;
until our cities are filled with God-inspired art.

In the 'Book of Psalms',
the songwriters were particularly sensitive to the times.

If times were great,
songs would be uplifting and personal.
"GREAT IS THE LORD!"

If times were rough,
more educational and congregational songs were written.
"WHERE IS THE LORD!?"

There were songs of correction,
songs of creation,
songs of thanks and songs of war.
Every praise and worship leader must follow the Hebrews.
Songs should only be sung in their proper season.

Asaph was one of the musical prophets David selected,
and spent his days writing Maschils:
teaching in music form.

When the Israelites were heading toward a spiritual decline,
Asaph wrote Psalm 78,
and reminded the people of the Jewish heritage.

Asaph took his role seriously as a prophet,
music was just the medium he expressed God through.

'Let the word of Christ dwell in you richly in all wisdom;
teaching and admonishing one another
in psalms and hymns and spiritual songs' Colossians 3:16

Music is the tool most of us use
to teach the word of God to each other.
So a burden is found on the songwriters,
as well as any artist.

If your content is repetitive and shallow,
the people's salvation will reflect that.

Sugarcoating is the bane of Christian creativity.
The reason why the world is moved by secular art,
and hardly touched by ours,
is because they can resonate with secular art.
The stories they tell are believable,
the characters they present are relatable.

Real people with real issues.
The moment our art comes becomes 'happy go lucky',
or hyper-spiritual,
we become unapproachable,
and our art ineffective.

If music is the teacher,
then the musicians,
as well as artists,
should be the most educated members in the body of Christ.
Above all, an artist must be well acquainted with scripture;
because your spiritual input
determines the people's spiritual outcome.

The people must elevate higher,
but you have to go deeper.

CHAPTER NINE

PAINTING PORTRAITS

THE OCEAN AND MOUNTAIN
EXPERIENCE

Many will admire the end product,
but will remain oblivious to the sacrifice it took to complete.

Remember Exodus 15:1-19,
where Moses sings a song,which could only be sung
because of his walk across the Red Sea.

Remember Deuteronomy 32:1-43,
where Moses sings another song,
and this time he sings about Adam
and the destruction of Gomorrah.

He never would have been able to sing of such things,
if he never climbed Mount Sinai.

Remember the ocean.
Remember the mountain.
You have to go through them both.
Remember your sacrifice.

Masterpieces do not just fall into our laps.
God needs to trust us with His gems.

Remember the New Testament,
how a great deal of it was written in prison.

Remember David,
how his journey to kingship was a strenuous one.

Remember his torturous life,
how he fought countless wars,
how he was soaked in bloodshed.
How he had to leave the city he ruled,
because his own children wanted him dead.

Still,
remember David,
who composed the most
intimate love songs ever written to God.

Remember the book of Psalms,
how it would have been an empty journal,
If David never felt pain.
Every artwork of value will cost you something:
Relationships.
Time.
Life choices.
Finances.

Sometimes an arm must be cut off for the chords to sound sweeter.
Anything that blocks success must drop off.

The deeper you dig, the richer your material.

Remember the darkness,
how God made light.

Remember Adam,
how God made Eve.

Remember the fall of man,
how God made Jesus.

In a moment of darkness,
creativity shines at its brightest.

Remember fasting,
and self-denial.
Remember solitude,
and alone time with God.
Remember His voice,
for quality is in the quiet.
Remember the message,
as it must change you first.

It is like painting portraits.
The subject walks into the room,
and you begin to paint the main features.

After a time, you spot features overlooked.
The smile.
The bone structure.
The light as it hits the face.

It is a time-consuming process,
but after the third or fourth session,
you fall in love with the subject.
You behold their beauty.
You acquaint yourself with their features.
Each brush stroke becomes more and more intimate.

Many will admire the end product,
but will remain oblivious to the sacrifice it took to complete.
Your very heart is spilt on the canvas,
and the journey has changed you in the process.

As artists,
we paint portraits of the King.
And even though many may marvel at the images we paint,
we witnessed His beauty first-hand.

CHAPTER TEN

DORCAS

THE IMPORTANCE OF SMALL BEGINNINGS

Everything looks fine from a bird's-eye view.
Zoom in close to see the broken homes.
You need not wait to see the end of the world,
just look outside of your window.

After the death of Jesus,
Peter calls it a day,
and goes back to his old day job,
fishing.

He fishes from dusk till dawn.
He catches nothing.

Resurrected Jesus walks by,
and tells Peter to cast his net on the right side of the ship.

Peter obeys,
and a hundred and fifty-three great fish splash out of the water.
The net becomes so heavy that Peter could hardly draw it out.

"Come and dine," Jesus says.

While eating some of the fish they caught,
Jesus says to Peter
"Do you love Me more than these?"
Peter in astonishment replies "of course I do, You know that."

Jesus then replies,
"then feed My sheep"

God has empowered our gifts and talents,
and we have benefitted greatly from them,
but Jesus persists in His request:
"Do you love Me more than your gifts?
Then use your gifts to serve My people."

The youths in tower blocks.
The shivering homeless.
The abused.

The forgotten.
The forsaken.
The refugee that seeks a welcome.
The addict who snorts intoxicants religiously.

The Bible says we are the restorers of society.

'They shall rebuild the old ruins, they shall raise up the former desolations, and they shall repair ruined cities, the desolations of many generations' *Isaiah 61:4*

What can we create
that would regenerate hoods and ghettos?

What can we create
that would warm the unloved?

What can we create
that would rehabilitate the unfortunate?

What can we create
that would end all gang wars?

How can we be a voice *for* them?
How can we be a voice *to* them?

To tell the fatherless they have worth.
To tell the abused they are beautiful.

You need not wait to find opportunities to evangelise,
opportunities lay at your doorstep.
We might want to change *the* world,
but we must first change *our* world.

My own community needs Jesus
before I preach Him overseas.

'Do not despise these small beginnings,
for the LORD rejoices to see the work begin' *Zechariah 4:10 [NLT]*

This is your incubational process,
your training ground.
If you want to affect the culture,
start small.
Start home.

Use the resources you *already* have.
Affect the people you *already* know.
Make art for an audience of ten,
as if you are making it for a crowd of a million.

A dead man is truly dead,
when his ideas die in the minds of the living.

If I consider God to be my lecturer,
then I must share my knowledge with others.
Bezalel was filled with extreme creative ability,
but Exodus 35:34 states that he was expected
to teach what he had learnt.

If you are amazing, make others equally amazing.
Education is essential.

There was a man named Robert Raikes
(editor of Gloucester Journal).
And during the time of his days,
education was reserved only for the rich.
Most children never knew how to read or write.
Most children worked thirteen-hour days in
factories with their parents.

Robert Raikes saw an issue.
He saw the downward spiral a child could possibly go down,
and thought prevention was better than cure.
He sought to give the children a good leg-up for the future,
by opening up a school in 1780.

The children worked in the factories from Monday to Saturday,
so Sunday could be the only designated day for study.

The Bible was the textbook of choice.
Christians were the teachers of choice.
Thus Sunday School was born,
the origin of public schooling.

We are a liberating faith,
not a restricting one.
We take expensive resources,
and distribute it out to the world for free.

'Go ye therefore, and teach all nations...' *Matthew 28:19 [KJV]*
If Jesus expects us to be the teacher of the nations,
then we must know something the world does not:
Kingdom Culture.

Essentially,
we are world leaders.

Our success is not defined by individual striving for greatness,
but in raising up the next generation of world-class creatives.

But the bigger picture can never be appreciated,
until we have noticed the smaller details.

'Counsel in the heart of man is like deep water; but a man of understanding will draw it out' *Proverbs 20:5*

Everyone has a 'deepness' about them.
Everybody has a calling
but not everyone can express his or her 'deepness' as well as we
can.

We are expected to nurture unsung legends.
We will see the hidden greatness in those around us,
and draw it out.

Acts 9:36-42 talks about a woman named Dorcas.

Dorcas was deeply adored in her community
because she made clothing for the financially stricken widows
around her.

When she died, the widows mourned her death so greatly,
they gathered enough faith to ask Peter to raise her back
from the dead.

Dorcas could have made art for the world,
but she made art for her people instead.

Oh, to be like Dorcas.

CHAPTER ELEVEN

FUNDS

Van Gough was told by his church to get a real job.

There is a reason why many churches lack creativity.
Artists and creatives are the most
misunderstood specimens in church.

Our callings are undervalued and at times disapproved of.

But then again,
some of us carry a shameful shade of self-importance.
Rogue artists.
Locking ourselves away from the crowd,
deeming our ministry more important than others.
Ever-creating,
attempting to single-handedly establish the
Kingdom of God with our craft;
without help.

Maybe that was just me.

Either way,
there must be a meeting in the middle.
The artist must *take the initiative* to
cooperate with their local church,
and the local church must understand
and appreciate the calling of an artist.

The local church needs to encounter culture,
and the artist has the understanding to do so.

The artist needs teaching, moral support and finances,
the local church can provide all three.

When the church was in its baby stages,
Acts 4:32-35 tells us that everybody had all things common.
Private possessions were sold,
and the proceeds were donated to the furtherance of the gospel.

The church was at one with their finances,

and it caused them to thrive in the early years.

Artists need funding.
There is only so much free music we can give away,
before we have no more money to record,
and our standards decay.

Every time you illegally download a gospel singer's album,
you greatly affect the quality of the follow-up.

Israelites saw the worth of artists.
1 Chronicles 15:16 says that musicians
were employed in the temple,
and were expected to make music night and day;
free from any other responsibility.

When the tabernacle was being built,
Moses asked the Israelites for an offering of materials.
Out of their free will,
everyone contributed greatly.

Do you know how much they gave?
Read Exodus 38:21-31.
Convert the weight of shekels into ounces,
and you will have a round up of £57 million.

Remember,
these men and women just came from
four hundred years of slavery,
but they still found the finances to give.

Moses had to restrict their abundant giving.
He sent out a law that prohibited
all future donations to the tabernacle.

When the temple was being built,
David outdid them all.

He wanted to see a place of beauty,

and was willing to put all of his money on the table.
The Bible said he gave three thousand talents of gold,
and seven thousand talents of silver.
In modern day money,
that is about £12.6 billion.

He could give £1.50 to every person on the planet,
and still have enough money to make the tabernacle.

£12.6 billion is enough to make something as exquisite
as the Taj Mahal, eighteen times over.

He stirred the princes to such a point,
that their offering combined with his
was an estimate of around £181 billion.

And that was just for the treasures *inside* the temple.
1 Kings 7:47 says that there were
additional goods to build the temple itself.
Scripture claims that the amount of treasure was so great,
That Solomon did not even bother to count it.

Many would see this as excessive,
but these men were not just funding an art project.
It was the financing of a gateway.
A portal where men can meet God.

Imagine the projects we could create
if we came together as a body.

Imagine if we had money circulating on a global scale.
What could we devise?

'Fulfil my joy by being likeminded, having the same love,
being of one accord, of one mind. Let nothing be done
through selfish ambition or conceit, but in lowliness of
mind let each esteem others better than himself. Let each of
you look out not only for his own interests, but also for the
interests of others' *Philippians 2:2-4*

Above finances,
we must have love.
Love to see others thrive,
love to bring to completion other people's projects.

If we gain excitement about our neighbour's ideas,
with the same excitement we have for our own,
a culture of innovation would surface in the church.

No more lone soldiers,
the church would now be a place of support for the artist.

And it is only when we get together as a body,
and *internally* flow innovation,
when we are fully ready to face outer darkness,
and wage war.

CHAPTER TWELVE

HIGH POWERS

'Hear, O Israel:
You are to cross over the Jordan today,
and go in to dispossess nations
greater and mightier then yourself,
cities great and fortified up to heaven' *Deuteronomy 9:1*

Never grumble about the apparent darkness in society.
Darkness is nothingness.

You cannot generate darkness.
You can only generate more light, or less light.

When darkness blankets the city,
it is due to our absence.

The church made its impact in Hollywood in the 1930s.
In a time of irresponsible filmmaking,
the church introduced the Hays Code,
a guideline for films.
It was set to protect the morality of moviegoers,
and overall national behaviour.

Violence in films was permitted,
but it never influenced you to do harm.
Romance was permitted,
but it never encouraged promiscuity.

This was not to restrict Hollywood's artistic freedom,
the church strongly believed in the freedom of speech.
But movies were now America's main force
for mass communication,
and were becoming too powerful to be left unsupervised.

A war broke between the church and the movie producers;
between cultural morality and financial gain.
The conflict continued for years.
Eventually, the producers won.
The church shut down their offices in 1966.
Three years later,

the first X-rated movie was released.

Since then,
Hollywood has stood for everything the church is against.
Violence is glorified,
immoral sex is advertised,
criminals are the good guys,
the concept of family is demoralised,
and Jesus is no more than a mere swear word.

Creativity executed correctly is influence,
and that is why Hollywood invests millions into it.
It persuades the thoughts of the masses.

Hollywood is not solely accountable.
Music moulds minds.
Games.
Literature.
Fashion.

And more times than not,
popular entertainment mocks Christian belief.

It is not a question of *why* we should be creative.
But what is the consequence if we are not?

'The Passion of the Christ' was released in cinemas in 2004;
telling the nations about salvation.
'The Da Vinci Code' came out two years later;
undermining Christ's sovereignty.

Your voice will always be challenged,
because this is a war on influence.

There was a Hebrew leader named Joshua.
God chose him to be the successor of Moses.
He was commanded to lead the Israelites
from Egypt to the Promised Land;
a land flowing with milk and honey.

But giants occupied the entire terrain,
and Joshua was expected to slay every single one of them.

Whenever God blesses His people,
he gives them territory.
TV stations.
Record labels.
Publishing houses.
Laboratories.
Technology firms.
Educational institutions.

The city is ours.
But yet, we must fight for it.

The more territory we own,
the more influence we carry.

Could we slay the giants up top;
the puppeteers of the culture?

We compete against the likes of Hollywood
for the world's attention.
Can we wage war on such a grand scale?
Can we contend against the spiritual darkness of the industry?
Could we overpower the *powers that be*?

Daniel 5:11 answers.
Demonic influences *infested* Babylonian government,
but Daniel was so spiritually in-tune,
that Nebuchadnezzar made him ruler over
all the magicians of Babylon.
He was connected to the highest power of them all.

Whether it is an occult or secret society,
they are no match.
We are indestructible.
Our creativity in the Spirit is a multicoloured sword,
and it slices to shreds the kingdom of darkness.

CHAPTER THIRTEEN

MIND GAMES

THE FORMING OF
WORLDVIEWS

'For we wrestle not against flesh and blood,
but against principalities,
against powers,
against the rulers of the darkness of this world,
against spiritual wickedness in high places' *Ephesians 6:12 [KJV]*

Never underestimate this fact:
we are not fighting against celebrities or governments.
We are not attacking physical beings,
we are wrestling with spiritual ones.
Our kitchen knife is no good in atomic war.
We must pray.

'God saw that the wickedness of man was great on the earth,
and that every imagination of the thoughts of his heart
was only evil continually' *Genesis 6:5 [KJV]*

God does not judge a generation by what they *do*,
but how they *think*.
He judges the mind;
the origin of all outward expression.

This is a battle for thoughts.

If you want a generation to believe a false idea,
slip it into a film,
or a song.
Create hundreds of songs and films just like it.
Release them continuously over a period of time,
until eventually the people believe the lie to be true,
and the idea becomes public opinion.

That is how we have all been raised.

Youth define themselves by the art they digest,
the music they listen to,
the clothes they wear,
the films they watch.
We are wrestling for the minds of the young.

The moral state of the next generation
is dependent on how well we fight today.

We were thrown in coliseums,
now our persecution is much more psychological.

We are not killed,
just kept silent.

Apologise.
Compromise.
Take it easy.

But our mandate does not allow us to do so.

'Casting down imaginations, and every high thing that exalteth
itself against the knowledge of God, and bringing into captivity
every thought to the obedience of Christ' *2 Corinthians 10:5 [KJV]*

Whatever art form we use,
we must use it to redeem imaginations.
We must revitalise thought lives.
Whether by word or by visual,
we must grab the people's attentions for brief moments,
and get them to think.

We are bringing into custody as many thoughts as possible.
That is the aim of the game,
but the conversion starts with us.

'Do not be conformed to this world,
but be transformed by the *renewing of your mind*' *Romans 12:2*

Picture your mind as a room.
What is hanging on the walls?
What is on the television?
What is the music being played?
Who is chilling on the sofa?
What are the conversations they keep?

Your mind is a room.
Jesus knocks on the door.
Can He come in?

We have all been slaves to the culture at some point.
We have all fell captive to its temptations.
But your mind is a room
where all of your creativity stems from.
What are your ideas sharing space with?

Daniel 1:8-20 tells us that during his three years of study,
Daniel was on a completely different diet
from all his colleagues.
He would eat vegetables,
while the rest would feast and fatten off the king's meat.
Yet, Daniel became the smartest student in the university.

Never follow the crowd.
The world may feast on Nebuchadnezzar's art,
but malnourished minds produce malnourished work.
Feed your mind with healthy material;
good music,
good books,
good conversations,
and you will produce work ten times richer.

Remember Joshua,
how he stood before the land of the giants,
and before going in to conquer,
God gives him assurance.

'No man shall be able to stand before you all the days of your
life… Be strong and very courageous, that you may observe to
do according to all the law… do not turn from it to the right
hand or the left, *that you may prosper wherever you go*… you
shall *meditate* in it day and night… for then you will make
your way *prosperous*, and then you will have *good success*'
Joshua 1:5-8

Success was not achieved by Joshua's fighting,
but by his *thinking*.

'Meditate on these things; give yourself entirely to them, *that your progress may be evident to all' 1 Timothy 4:15*

Joshua discovered the power of meditation,
long before any modern-day entrepreneur.

There is a reward in holy thinking.
There is a blessing if we hold every thought captive.

But thought life normally goes unsupervised.
Nobody sees it,
so we allow our minds to wander,
and leave it to be a playground for immorality.

God is not mocked.
He hears our thoughts loud as if we shout them on rooftops.
He will reward us accordingly.

Your standing with God equals your standing in the industry.
Never expect elevation in your arena if your prayer life is dead.
Surround yourself with the Word of God.
Eat it up and meditate on it daily.

That is how you achieve success God's way.

The practices of society are enticing,
but Deuteronomy 18:9 warns us that when we tred new soil,
we must never worship the gods of that culture.

The higher you arise,
the stronger the temptations.
but do not give in,
you cannot afford it.

Sin is a silencer.
It stops you from speaking against it.

It robs you of your boldness.
It pollutes the flow of empowerment on your life.

'He who covers his sins will not prosper, but whoever
confesses and *forsakes* them will have mercy' *Proverbs 28:13*

Be transparent.
Confess and forsake.

This is a wrestle,
but never run into the heat of the battle without preparation.
Spiritual preparation is the only guarantee to victory.

Before Joshua even thought to conquer land,
Exodus 33:11 tells us that he constantly
worshipped in the tabernacle.

He sought to know his God
before he handled God's business.

Before considering war,
consider praying.
You can create until the sun goes down,
but wars are only won on your knees.

If you fail to pray,
you have already lost.

As a matter of fact,
the potential of creative power we have inside of us
can only be unlocked by prayer and fasting.

The battlefield is in the mind.
Your only weapon is the Spirit.
Your only ammunition is prayer and fasting.

CHAPTER FOURTEEN

SELAH

Father,
God of creation.
Thank You for such a gift,
And entrusting me to fulfil such a task.

It is an honour to be called by You,
and to birth Your intangible thoughts.
Forgive me for every time I underestimated Your creativity,
and esteemed my own.

Renew my mind.
I unlearn everything to be taught by You.
Allow me to have the mind of Christ,
so I can explore Your deepness,
and create works fit for a King.

I consider no invention to be my own,
but now I am a steward of *Your* ideas.

Give me observant eyes.
Help me to see as You see.
Allow me to see which was,
which is,
and which is to come,
so I can guide Your people effectively.

Give me ears to hear Your voice.
Teach me how to listen.
Tell me when to start.
Tell me when to stop.
Let me be sensitive to Your direction.

I pray You give me labouring hands.
Enhance my skill.
Whatever these hands work upon,
let it prosper.

Finally, give me a willing heart.
Whatever I create,
help me to speak from my heart to Yours.
Help me to touch the hearts of a people,
Whether they are many or few.
Let no sin stop the flow of our synergy.
Purify me.

Shine through the works of my hands.
Shine with the brightness of the Sun.
Let my work be a bridge between You and man.

Whether big or small,
I pray You are pleased with my efforts.
I pray my works give You glory.

These things I ask in Your name, Jesus.
Amen.

CHAPTER FIFTEEN

VIVAS IN DEO

"I come that they may have life,
and that they may have it more abundantly"
- Jesus *(John 10:10)*

No one on earth can stop our cry.
None can quench this joy inside.
This song we sing both far and wide:
"VIVAS IN DEO"
"VIVAS IN DEO"

Cities marvel at our praise,
and turn from all their wicked ways,
the day they hear our glorious praise:
"VIVAS IN DEO"
"VIVAS IN DEO"

David brings the Ark of the Covenant into the city,
and the whole nation erupts into dance.
The sounds of tambourine bangs fill the air.
The presence of the Lord is back in Jerusalem.

The word 'praise'
has seven definitions in Hebrew.

The first is

YAHDAH *(yaw-daw')*

which means to thrust your hands up to the air in submission,
furiously, as if you are throwing a javelin into the enemy's camp.

The second is

TOWDAH *(to-daw')*

which is like YAHDAH,
but instead of submission,
you lift your hands in thanksgiving.

The third is

BARAKH *(baw-rak')*

which means to kneel down.

The fourth is

TEHILLAH *(teh-hil-law')*

to sing a song spontaneously .

The fifth is

ZAMAR *(zaw-mar')*

to play music,
not necessarily with instruments,
but with the clapping of your hands.

The sixth is

SHABACH *(shaw-bakh')*

to shout at the top of your lungs.

God is a God of energy.
He is extremely expressive.

David knew this,
and that is why David did all the praises he could.

He danced.
He danced hard.
David danced so hard that his girdle fell off.

David danced so hard, he was praising in his city naked,
and did not even think to civilise himself.

The seventh praise is called

HALAL *(haw-lal')*.

It is where we get the word 'Hallelujah' from.
It means to shine or be exuberant.
It also means to act crazy and foolish.

David did HALAL.
He praised God like a madman,
irrespective of who was watching.

What would cause a king to act so out of character in public?
He remembered his roots.
He remembered when he was the unloved teenager
looking after sheep.

And now he is a king,
bringing the presence of God back into his city.

That deserves a praise break.

Imagine we collectively began to create for Christ.

Imagine we spoke of His love poetically on the trains.
Imagine we proclaimed His gospel on billboards.
Imagine we showed off His vibrancy in our music.
Imagine we displayed His story in cinemas.

Imagine if we went all out.
Imagine the shift we would see in our culture.

But who are we
that we should feel so free?

Who are we
to usher in the presence of God into our cities?

Who are we
to be cloaked in such liberty?

We are nobodies,
yet God knights us the unknown kings of this age.

Hallelujah.

We will slay giants,
but to know that through our warfare,
our cities could experience God's presence,
we fight with smiles on our faces.

We do it with joy,
because the life we live,
is life in its abundance.
And it would be our honour
to take our brightness,
and light up the world with it.

We are enriching lives with the art we make.
Our vibrancy doth liberate.
And thus our song will yet suffice:
"VIVAS IN DEO"
Alive in Christ

CHAPTER SIXTEEN

ART
& DESTRUCTION

'By the rivers of Babylon, there we sat down,
yea, we wept when we remembered Zion' *Psalm 137:1*

Jerusalem is in ruins.
Jerusalem is bare.
And all of the Israelites walk into this strange city
in shackles and chains.
Slaves to the new world power.

Welcome to Babylon.

David sought to establish a temple,
but Solomon built it.
A monument.
A statement to say that God has a home,
and His home is in Jerusalem.

'The house to be built for the LORD must be exceedingly
magnificent, famous and glorious throughout all countries'
– David *(1 Chronicles 22:5)*

Set up on a high hill so the world could see.
The temple on Mount Moriah,
later named Mount Zion.

God appeared to Solomon,
and made him a deal in 1 Kings 9:3-9.
If Solomon and other kings kept their integrity,
then God would sustain the temple for generations.

But if they swayed,
God would take back the land He had given them,
and make the temple a spook story to surrounding nations.

Solomon agreed.
But idolatry crept in,
and corrupted the king.
Him, and all of the kings that followed after him.

Idolatry is subtle.
It creeps in unsuspected.
One minute you are making art for God,
next, you are making a god out of art.

'They lavish gold out of the bag, and weigh silver on the scales;
they hire a goldsmith, and he makes it a god; they prostrate
themselves, yes, they worship' *Isaiah 46:6*

We have a tendency to worship the works of our own hands.
Israel has a track record for that.
Moses made a sculpture that healed anyone who looked at it.
Read Numbers 21:8-9.
But by the time we reach 2 Kings 18:4,
it had to be destroyed because the people burnt incense to it.

Creativity is power.
It can be used for good.
It can be used for bad.

God understands what we feel
when we connect with our creations.
It is a God-given trait.
He feels the same about us.

But when our mind is off God,
and on our talents,
idolatry creeps.

The Israelites' hearts were far from God.
But still,
they saw the temple as the pride of Jerusalem.
They thought that because the temple was still intact,
it meant God was cool with their sin.
Giving them a freedom pass to continue their immoral living.

They preferred the temple of the Lord,
over the Lord of the temple.

Loving the architecture,
loathing the Architect.
Then 587 B.C happened.
The Babylonians invaded Israel.
They came with torches,
and burnt the whole city down.
The Israelites are taken in as slaves,
and the temple is smashed to pieces.

Mount Zion,
a place that astonished the greatest men,
is now rubble.
It is now a statement to the nations:
"God has left the building."

A heart *for* God creates great works of art.
A heart *against* God creates great works of destruction.

It is either a tremendous rise,
or a tremendous fall.
This is what you get when God is with you.
This is what you get when He is gone.

Since then,
men have tried to rebuild the temple,
but every time they build it back up,
enemies keep breaking it back down.

Would you like to know what is on the top of Mount Zion now?
It is the Dome of the Rock,
a Muslim monument.

God was not joking.

And thus Solomon's psalm rings with greater clarity:
'unless the LORD builds the house,
they labour in vain who build it' *Psalm 127:1*

This is Kingdom business,
and Kingdom business is serious business.
Whatever we create,
must be ordained and sustained by the King.
Unless God is at the core of it,
our projects are pointless,
And can only result in embarrassment.

To avoid destruction,
never allow art to replace the anointing.
Never let aesthetic perfection substitute God's power.

The Babylonians took it all.
The treasure.
The art.
The artists.

A generation of musicians were held captive.
And in a strange city,
they were all expected to sing the songs they knew from back
home.

They weep,
when they remember Zion.

'How shall we sing the LORD's song in a foreign land?
If I forget you, O Jerusalem, let my right hand forget its skill!
If I do not remember you,
let my tongue cling to the roof of my mouth -
if I do not exalt Jerusalem above my chief joy' *Psalm 137:4-6*

They were in chains,
held captive in a culture that cared little for their faith.
But as the psalmist says,
if I ever forget where I came from,
let me forget how to create.

Creativity is just a supplement to worship.
It helps sustain us
as we reside in this city.

But if we ever lose heart,
forget who we are,
and become slaves in this decaying culture,
this modern day Babylon,
for Christ's sake,
let our hands forget their skill.

Let us never make art again.

VOLUME III

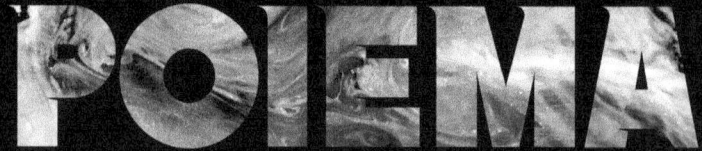

THE PORTRAITS

CHAPTER ONE

FALLEN

'How art thou fallen from heaven,
O Lucifer, son of the morning!
How art thou cut down from the ground,
and dist weaken the nations!
For thou hast said in thine heart,
I will ascend in heaven,
I will exalt my throne above the stars of God:
I will sit also upon the mount of the congregation,
in the sides of the north:
I will ascend above the heights of the clouds;
I will be like the most high.

Yet thou shalt be brought down to hell,
to the sides of the pit' *Isaiah 14:12-15 [KJV]*

Ezekiel 28 writes about him,
and says he was perfect in his beauty.

His body incrusted in jewels.
The sum of awe-inspiring instruments.
The voice of an angel.
His name was Lucifer,
the Son of the Morning.

As close to the throne of Heaven as any creature could be.
He was the covering of God.
A cloak.
The jewels he was emblazed with,
reflected the light of God's brightness.
His beauty and talent exceeded any angel in Heaven.
But beauty and talent was not enough.

Venom poisons Lucifer's heart,
and pride pushes him to self-promotion.

He no longer wants to reflect God,
he wants to be God.
He no longer wants to serve,
he wants to be served.

A war erupts in Heaven,
and Lucifer and a third of the angels
are kicked out of Heaven in a lightning flash.

He screams in agony in the lowest hell,
and burns from without and within.
wallowing in darkness.

From the highest mountain,
to the lowest pit.

He has fallen.

He looks up at the heavens with a sickening arrogance,
and foams at the mouth in rage.

A hate for God,
a hate for the things of God.

He then hears in the echoes of space,
God's plans of The Unthinkable.

A new art piece.
A creation more beautiful than anything He has made before.
A self-portrait that would be given divine rule.

They would be kings.

Everything Satan wanted to possess.
Everything Satan wanted to be.

And in the presence of devils, man was made.

The attributes of God lovingly wrapped in flesh and bone.
The Mastermind's greatest work.

Satan's mission remained operational.
He still wanted to be equal with God,
and he sought to spit in God's face,

by destroying His image.

Satan sought to poison man,
and get them on his side.
by filling them with the same poison that corrupted him:

self-worship.

CHAPTER TWO

ORION

THE SEARCH FOR
TRUE SUPERSTARDOM

'Then the serpent said to the woman,
"You will not surely die.
For God knows that in the day you eat of it
your eyes will be opened,
and you will be like God,
knowing good and evil"' *Genesis 3:4-5*

He seductively whispered sweet lies into our ears,
promising enlightenment.
Taking the power we already had,
and selling it back to us at a cheaper price.

He said by eating the forbidden fruit,
God will no longer be the middleman between us and greatness.
So we bit into his lie,
and mankind has rotted ever since.

From age to age,
this curse has crippled the greatest of men.
From kings to everyday civilians,
we have all bowed down to the temptations of the three:
POWER.
FAME.
FORTUNE.
And have sought to exchange our very soul to acquire it all.

We yearn to be noticed by the masses.
To stroll on red carpets,
and sip champagne with the rich and famous.

We yearn to shine bright.
We yearn to have our name in lights.
We yearn superstardom.

We have become overwhelmed with ego.
No longer in the image of God,
but bearing resemblance to Lucifer,
with minds of self-worship.

Governments have bowed down to his lies.
His trickery has deceived the entire globe,
so much so that 2 Corinthians 4:4 calls him
"The god of this world".

Satanism:
The first religion every man partakes in.
We need not give our consent.
We were all born into it.

1 John 2:16 speaks of the unholy trinity of this worldwide belief:

THE LUST OF THE FLESH
(Self-pleasure)

THE LUST OF THE EYE
(Materialism)

THE PRIDE OF LIFE
(Selfish ambition)

We were all slaves to his religion and rule;
all of us,
until Jesus came.

Our freedom from Satan's rule,
depended on the events that took place in Matthew 4.

Jesus is thirty years old and unknown.
No one has heard Him speak,
and He is yet to begin His mission.

Still,
He secludes Himself in Arabian deserts,
fasting for forty days;
preparing Himself
for the biggest shake-up in humanity since Genesis.

Up until this point,
Satan had every man of power under his influence.
But one of his biggest fears,
was that men would one day realise,
that submission to Satan is not compulsory.
The earth could run sufficiently without him.

Jesus poses the biggest threat,
for He pursues world domination,
without having a speck of sin in Him;
giving Satan nothing to bargain with.

He persists nonetheless.

At the end of the forty day fast,
Jesus faces temptation,
And battles with challenging thoughts.

At the end of Matthew 3,
God confirms that Jesus is the Son of God.
But in Matthew 4,
Satan proposes three temptations,
beginning the first two with the phrase
"*IF* you are the Son of God..."
questioning His sovereignty.

The first temptation was to turn stones into bread.
Jesus resisted.
The second temptation was to throw Himself off the temple,
so angels would catch Him.
Jesus resisted once more.

Satan's frustration overcame him.
He could not allow this man to succeed in His efforts.

Then it clicked.
Satan had the temptation that had the
entirety of mankind in the balance.

What was Jesus' mission?
What was the *one* thing He spoke about?
What did He say He was coming to establish?
The Kingdom.

Matthew 4:8-9 tells us that Satan took Him to a high mountain,
and showed Him all the great nations of the world.

Jesus saw it.
Every creed,
every nation,
every king
from every age,
bowing down to Him.

The Indians,
the Australians,
the Norwegians,
the Germans,
the English,
the Egyptians.

Fame beyond fathom.
Everything Jesus ever wanted
handed to Him on a plate.
And He could have it all,

right there and then,
without ever having to go to the cross.

He did not need to have nails pushed into His hands,
or have religious leaders spit in His face.
He did not need to be unloved,
and face ridicule by the masses.

He was provided with the easy way out.
All Jesus had to do,
was bow down to the god of this world.

If Jesus succumbed,
The Bible would have ended at Matthew 4:10.
We never would have heard the Beatitudes,
and Salvation would have been nothing more than a fairy tale.

But Jesus did not want to share.
Jesus wanted it all.
He saw the bigger picture,
and endured persecution.
He carried the cross for us,
and inherited the earth legally.

It is only when He overcame His biggest temptation,
when He was able to teach us about The Kingdom.
It is only when He denied fame when His ministry started.

Now, all power belongs to Him.

Satan failed by self-promotion.
Jesus succeeded by self-denial.

Revelation 12:17 says that Satan is so sickened by Jesus' success,
that he seeks to kill anybody that looks remotely like Him.
That is where we come in.

Our biggest temptations
are just before our biggest breakthroughs.

And sometimes we settle prematurely,
exchanging kingship with compromise,
becoming ineffective to those who really need us.

Solomon was wiser than all,
yet he wrote Ecclesiastes,
a book that documents his fall.

He had curiosity to discover everything under the sun,
but he called it "soar travail".
He was an industrious man,
and a builder of many cities,
but his conclusion was that "all is vanity".

He sought wisdom excessively until he lost sight of God,
and considered his efforts to be of great consequence.

'In much wisdom is much grief:
and he who increases knowledge
increases sorrow' *Ecclesiastes 1:18*

'...Nor be overly wise:
why should you destroy yourself?' *Ecclesiastes 7:16*

'...Of making books there is no end;
and much study is wearisome to the flesh' *Ecclesiastes 12:12*

The creativity we have,
is creativity for *this* life.
Our creativity is of no use in the next life,
and is not guaranteed longevity after we are gone.

The gift works for us,
we do not work for the gift.
The creativity we have is to be enjoyed by ourselves and others.

It is possible to be the most creative being on the planet,
no doubt,
but to whom much is given,

much is required.
Why would you *want* to be the world's most creative person?
What will you do with all the power you carry?
If your aim is to shine the light of Christ,
then pursue creative excellence at all costs.
But if your aim is to be a legendary figure,
And to chase immortality on earth through your works of art,
then you are making an unnecessary gamble
and a vain decision.

Creativity is a beautiful gift,
but it is not the be all and end all.
What is the point of being an amazing artist
if you are a lousy husband?
What is the point being a genius
if you have forgotten the people you are to celebrate your genius
with?

Ah, what pleasure it is,
to be so free that there is no cap on your creative output,
but so balanced your gifts do not overcome you.

This is not to say fame is sin,
but it is not the objective.

After Jesus' temptation,
Matthew 4:24 tells us that fame *followed* Him.
Swarms of people flocked to hear Him teach.
But because He denied fame in private previously,
He did not used it as a luxury,
but as a responsibility to spread the Gospel on a wider scale;
so when He lost favour in the public eye,
it never affected *Him* as a person.

Humility before elevation.

We never have to seek for fame,
we are famous already.
The King of kings knows who we are,
and He is our biggest fan.

He has read every book,
heard every song,
watched every play before we have even *thought* of them.
We never need to sell our souls for handclaps and pats on the back.
The only "well done" we need to hear is from the Lord.

When God pours His creative power upon us,
which He will,
it will gather great amounts of attention.
The test lies in what we do with the fame that is given.

'Those who are wise shall *shine* like the brightness of the firmament, and those that turn many to righteousness *like the stars* forever and ever' *Daniel 12:3*

When the spotlight hits,
we have a greater responsibility to feed the nations.
Our success is in our serving.

That is true superstardom.

CHAPTER THREE

BEAUTY'S SAKE

'But now, O LORD, You are our Father;
we are the clay, and You our potter;
and all we are the work of Your hand' *Isaiah 64:8*

That is justification.
That is sanctification.
That is glorification.

There is a reason for the colours of the rainbow,
and the oozing vibrancy of the galaxies.

Beauty's sake.
He made all things beautiful for beauty's sake.

And we are His masterpiece.

'For the LORD takes pleasure in His people: He will beautify the
humble with salvation.' Psalm 149:4

Sin made us completely repulsive.
The Artist's anger was upon us,
but God made another Masterpiece,
and placed His anger *on that work* instead.
We are now seen as right in His sight.
That is justification.

We are saved from God's wrath,
but now He places us on the table;
and even though horrifically disfigured,
He chips away at unwanted sins,
until we resemble the image of His Son.
That is sanctification.

It is a painful process,
but we never move,
neither do we think to mar ourselves again with sin;
for it slows down the process of us being finished works.
And like any artist,
God finds no pleasure in seeing His work incomplete.

He treats our lives as fashion designers do with expensive material.
He separates us for His most desired purposes.
He makes us a *cut above* the rest.
That is what holiness means.

Revelation 2:7
Revelation 2:11
Revelation 2:17
Revelation 2:26-28
Revelation 3:5
Revelation 3:12
Revelation 3:21

Jesus guarantees weighty promises
to those who endure sanctification,
and overcome the culture.

He concludes in Revelation 21:7
"He who overcomes shall inherit all things,
and I will be his God, and he shall be My son"

That is glorification.

The Bible only gives one chapter
to account the creation of the universe,
and allows the rest of the book to account the creation of man.

The universe was just a side project for God.
Matthew 24:35 says that heaven and earth will pass away,
but Revelation 21:1 says a *new* heaven and earth will be made.
We are the main attraction.
We are the only created beings that will be exported
into God's new movement of artwork.

Your ministry is not as important as your salvation.
God does not value your art,
as much as He values your heart.

Ephesians 2:10 says that we are

POIEMA.

It is where we get the word 'poetry'.
It means we are His workmanship.
Out of all the things we seek to create,
our greatest work of art is our own lives.

Downfalls.
Successes.
Joys.
Heartaches.
He makes grand stories out of us.
Poetically crafted.
Motion pictures that the angels marvel at.

Replicas of God,
embodiments of His Kingdom.

"The Kingdom of God does not come with observation; Nor will
they say, 'See here!' or 'See there' For indeed,
The Kingdom of God is *within you*" – Jesus *(Luke 17:20-21)*

God's rule starts from the inside of us,
and radiates out into our world.

This is not simply religion,
we are in a *relationship* with the Artist.

We are the physical representations of a *partially* visible God.

We can see His hands
(that is His works).
We can see His body,
(that is His church).
But His face is hidden,
and it is our life long task to seek it,
and reflect it.

'Blessed are the pure in heart:
for they shall see God' *Matthew 5:8*

CHAPTER FOUR

KINGDOM

THE RISE OF THE CREATIVE
CHURCH

Last scene.

2 Chronicles 5:12-14.
Solomon gathers Israel's finest musicians
for the temple's opening ceremony.

They played with the trumpets,
the cymbals,
the psalteries,
the harps.
They sung aloud with their vocal chords,
and each instrument orchestrated sounds of heavenly beauty.

But,

it was only when the musicians and singers were as one,
and made one sound before the Lord,
that we witness the crescendo.

Scripture says that a thick cloud filled the temple,
with a potency so powerful that the choir could no longer sing.
It was the glory of the Lord.

Their oneness caught the Master's attention.

Individually, we carry weight,
but what happens when we are as one?

What happens when we drop off our selfish ambition,
and in unison strive to experience God's glory?

No more denominations.
Just Kingdom.

'This gospel of The Kingdom will be preached in all the world
as a witness to all the nations, and then the end will come'
Matthew 24:14

There will come a time when our hard work will pay off,
and all of our prayers,
all of our fasting,
all of our weeping,
will all make sense.

We will see our Creator face to face,
and we will experience His limitless creativity first hand.

We can only imagine
the countless universes that would unravel before our very eyes;
all with their own creatures and laws;
no day being remotely alike.
Everyday,
for the rest of eternity.

Possibly He will show us how He makes such creations.
Possibly He will give us the same power.
Possibly.

But for the time being,
we rise.

We will establish The Kingdom everywhere we go.
From the tower blocks to the mud huts.
From the streets of Brooklyn,
to the igloos of the Arctic.

We will make sure the earth is filled with God's influence.

So when the King comes back,

we will hear "well done".

We have been faithful over little,

now He will make us rulers over much.

Blessed are the meek,

for they shall inherit the earth.

THERISEOFTHECREATIVECHURCH.COM